Journey of a Longing Heart

A Jewish Kid's Search for God

AKIVA COHEN

Journey of a Longing Heart
Akiva Cohen

First Edition, 2024

ISBN: 978-2-9134-4498-0

Images Credit
Pieta de Michelangelo Vaticano credit to Stanislav Traykov Day of Judgment credit to Public Domain, https://commons.wikimedia.org/w/index.php?curid=16143987 Mt. Sinai credit to Shutterstock.com

A match head is only the size of a few grains of sand but when it ignites darkness has to flee

Contents

Chapter 1

Beginnings

My grandparents hailed from Russia on my mother's side, and from Lithuania on my father's. Both couples arrived in Johannesburg, South Africa, in the early part of the twentieth century in the wake of the pogroms and before the Holocaust. One of our relatives later published a family history that chronicled the names of our Lithuanian family members who, sadly, perished in the Holocaust. My father, Kenneth Eric Cohen, *z'l* (of blessed memory) told us what became a legendary family story that shaped our sense of ancestral glory. Our uncle *Rufka* had yanked two Cossacks from their horses when they trotted into his Jewish *shtetl* in Lithuania. If my father had exaggerated that account, that did not in any way diminish its impact upon us. Surely, there was a kernel of truth in it. There were more "Uncle Rufka stories," after he too had emigrated to South Africa. One such story concerns how he noticed two African farm hands straining to lift a sagging mealie (corn) sack onto a cart. He marched over to them and "with one hand" chucked the sack onto the cart, exhorting the laborers to work more diligently. That was no big deal for the man who had yanked the Cossacks from their horses, reinforcing our esteem for our heroic ancestor's apparent supernatural strength.

My mother, Hilary, had chronicled our family photographs behind protective plastic covers; the earliest of which are scenes of our lives in South Africa. She wrote captions below many of the white-framed polaroids in her meticulous handwriting. My earliest photo is of my infant frame, bound to the back of our African "nanny," going about her daily work at our home in a Johannesburg suburb. I'll return to South Africa later, paralleling my actual return as a young man.

In 1964, as a four-year-old, I arrived with my parents, my older sister, and my younger brother to Toronto, Canada. I was a loner growing up and life was full of enchantment. I enjoyed spending time in the solitude of our backyard with its towering pine trees. One of my earliest memories is the anxiety I felt over losing life's sense of wonder. On a sunny Canadian winter day, my internal needle pointing true north, I headed out our front door in my hooded snowsuit, gloves, and boots, and lay on my back in the sparkling snow. In the solitude of that bright day, I began to wave my arms and legs into a snow angel. It was my way of sending a signal, imploring whatever celestial power was up there to take notice of my plea and help me retain at least a vestige of my soul's fading enchantment.

Growing up, my sibs and I attended *Holy Blossom Temple* until our *Bar* and *Bat Mitzvahs*. We attended once-a-week Shabbat school lessons as a family and cultural requirement. My brother survived the temple services by inserting a comic book into the *Siddur* (prayer book). My brother and I were glad when we were finally free of this commitment after our *Bar Mitzvahs*. We did, however, continue as a family to attend the High Holiday services. I enjoyed hearing the deep tones of the organ, and seeing the choir in their flowing robes prepare to ascend the *bimah* to chant a Hebrew liturgical piece. I also received a spiritual impartation from an older woman who taught us occasionally. "The most important thing you can do," she intoned, "is to pray the *Shema* before you go to bed." I took her words to heart and would regularly recite, *Shema Yisrael, Adonai, Eloheinu, Adonai Echad,* ("Hear, O Israel, The Lord our God, the Lord is one") before going to sleep each night. I remain grateful to my parents for strengthening our sense of Jewish heritage through our connection with Reform Judaism.

If my Bar Mitzvah was not a meaningful coming-of-age ritual, rock'n'roll was the portal to a new plane of existence that deeply impacted me. After purchasing the Beatles'

Abbey Road album, I made my way to our den with it. My parents had a sophisticated stereo system lodged into dark walnut shelving—its two speakers on opposite shelves. I carefully positioned the stereo needle onto the LP groove. The introductory riff of *Come Together* was revelatory—its mesmerizing drum roll sounding from the right speaker, and the guitar and bass riffs from the left, ending with the soft clang of the cymbals, interspersed with a vocal, "*shhhhh.*" My soul was transported to a heightened consciousness. Record covers were a thing back then. I loved unfolding the album cover of *Sgt. Pepper's Lonely Hearts Club Band* to see the fab-four staring up at me.

If the Beatles brought a measure of light into my life, Alice Cooper gave entrance to the darkness. Drawn to his music, and intrigued by his top hat and smudged eye-liner theatrical appearance, I decided to tape his glossy album insert to my bedroom wall: a photograph of him *hanging from a noose*. My dad, looking at the poster, humbly said to me, "Maybe you should take that down, we've had some bad luck since you put it up." I'm not sure what troubles he was referring to, but whatever he meant, I blew it off at the time. A darker influence came by way of reading, *The Exorcist.* I vividly recall the visceral fear I felt at night—trying to block out the vision of the demon-possessed girl rotating her head 360 degrees. My sense of dread was so palpable that I was barely able to flee from my bedroom, down the carpeted hallway, to the bathroom. Later in life, I came to understand the reality of the spiritual world, one that is inhabited by both good and evil forces.

My elementary to Middle school years were turbulent and my lack of inner peace drove me to be disruptive in class. As a result, my parents, seeking to help me, removed me from the public education system and transferred me into the heart of an all-boys, private school.

The school's sports track and expansive soccer field led to its impressive old-world buildings. Their website currently advertises, "*Men of Character, from Boys of Promise.*" I think I was the first *Jewish* boy of promise to grace its halls. During my second year there, another Jewish friend enrolled, which made me feel a strong kinship with him. I had an ambivalent feeling towards our uniforms—grey pants, white dress shirts, and dark green blazers with the school's emblem—but did think it was impressive that we wore "house" ties.

As I was walking down a hallway one day, I saw the school *prefect* approaching me. They were older students and wore a special pin on their lapels to indicate their exalted status. I began to prepare my greeting, excited to be able to encounter him in the hallway. As he passed me, without deigning to make eye contact, he barked out of the side of his mouth, *Kike.* Even though I could not have told you then what that epithet meant, I knew *from the way that he said it* that it was a slur, and somehow related to the fact that he knew that I was *Jewish.* A category that he clearly thought was not supposed to mess up the clear lines of the school's various Anglo 'houses.' It was one of my first encounters with anti-Semitism and seemed so inexplicable, especially since all he knew of me was that I was Jewish. He had probably picked up the slur from his parents. I felt a certain invisibility during those years that allowed me to slip in and out of life as a sort of observer, and so although it was an unpleasant experience, I simply blew it off as yet another eccentric experience related to my ethnicity. In later years when I recalled, and better understood what had transpired in that encounter, I felt a surge of anger and wished that I could go back in time and confront that *prefect.* Now, I simply feel pity for him, and people like him who need to affirm their sense of racial superiority by demeaning those of another race—which ironically indicates their moral inferiority.

After these markers of my coming-of-age years, I attempted to re-enchant my life through magic and the paranormal. As a young teen, I had written a poem about a magician that was published in a Toronto newspaper. It was about how magicians deceive us, and how we agree to suspend our unbelief to enjoy their illusions. My connection with magic came to me by way of Niagara Falls, justly considered one of the wonders of the world. Less than two hours from our home, the proximity of the Falls allowed our family to easily drive there for occasional visits. Who has stood by its precipice, watching its strong current disappear over its edge, and not sensed its majestic roar? Or, who has not felt one's frailty standing in a hooded raincoat from behind a cavern *on the inside* of the falls as its water tumbles down a few feet away? As much as the power and beauty of the falls captivated me as a child, I was equally impacted by my visits to the *Houdini Magical Hall of Fame* on the Falls' commercial strip. The museum contained many of the handcuffs Houdini had escaped from, as well as his iconic water torture cell. The store sold magic kits, and other items of interest, such as, 'Kreskin's Krystal.' Named after *the Amazing Kreskin.* It came with a glass cube and a glass ball attached to a delicate metal chain. Lying on my bedroom carpet, I practiced holding the crystal over its base—marked with "Yes," in one direction, and "No," in the other—causing the ball to swing in whichever direction my mind desired it to swing. I had convinced myself that even the most imperceptible movement of my hand had nothing to do with the ball's kinetic wonder as it began to swing. I'm still not sure it didn't!

I also became fascinated with the Israeli mentalist, Uri Geller. I discovered him on TV and was amazed to watch him ask people for their keys, rub them lightly with his thumb and forefinger, and see them melt like wax before he handed them back to their owner, completely bent out of shape. I became such a fan that I bought his LP. It was a recording of his mesmerizing, even if somewhat comic, voice accompanied by ambient music. I listened to it intently in my room. *"Bend, bend, bend,"* he declared, as I gently rubbed my house key with all the mystic concentration I could muster. (You guessed it, my attempts at rubbing my keys until they began to 'melt' and bend never succeeded). I noticed that Geller was visiting Toronto at a given downtown location and went to meet him in person. I handed him his album to sign. He smiled, pleasantly surprised, "A real fan," he said in his thick Israeli accent, and proceeded to bend my housekey by gently rubbing it, exactly as I had seen him do on TV.

After "doing my time" at the private boys' school my parents restored me to public school for grade nine. The next year I turned fourteen and entered High School. Music continued to play a huge role in my life. I'd put my over-the-ear headphones on and blast Stevie Wonder's *Inner Visions* to feel the funk and anger of the inner city street and Stevie's inimitable voice. I felt the earth move when I'd groove to Carol King singing, *"I feel the earth move under my feet."* Cat Stevens's baritone voice captivated me and caused me to reflect on his lyrics as he strummed his acoustic guitar and entranced my soul. One line, in particular, from *Oh Very Young* made a deep impression on me.

Oh very young, what will you leave us this time?
You're only dancin' on this earth for a short while.
And though your dreams may toss and turn you now
They will vanish away like your dad's best jeans
Denim blue, faded up to the sky
And though you want them to last forever
You know they never will.

Those lines pierced my heart. I loved my blue jeans, and the thought that they'd wear out one day and I'd have to get rid of them touched the angst I felt towards my mortality. A poem I wrote in those days took up the theme of the earth grabbing at our clay feet as we dance upon it—trying to pull us down to our graves. Another poem I wrote as a teenager is still etched into my memory.

One cold dark December night,
in my rearview mirror:
a red flashing light.
A siren grows louder from behind.
An ambulance zooms by.
I exhale and calm my mind.

I recall explaining the poem to a close high school friend. I knew that death was on our heels and would eventually catch up with us. But I was glad for a reprieve—the ambulance was coming for someone else, at least for now. Those same themes about the fleeting nature of life were in the poems and lyrics I wrote. I recorded one of my songs on a cassette tape in my basement with a group of friends. It was called, "Searching." *Downtown bums became my friends, not just buts of life's burned-out ends ... Searching, but I don't know where I'm going ...* and on it went about my search for life's meaning. That line in my song was inspired by T.S. Eliott's *The Love Song of J. Alfred Prufrock.* "*To spit out all the butt-ends of my days and ways?*" Mr. Smith, our High School English and Drama teacher—the only teacher who made a life-long impression on me—had told us about the profundity of good poetry, Michelangelo's art, and Springsteen's lyrics. All of which would play a significant role in my search for meaning. For the latter, I recall playing the harmonica melody for *Thunder Road* and belting out in my best raspy Jersey-accented voice, "*The screen door slams, Mary's dress waves. Like a vision, she dances across the porch as the radio plays,*" as I strummed my amped-up Gibson in the lounge area outside my basement room. A song that I recorded in a friend's studio around that time was called, "The Wind is Gonna Blow Through It." The song's chorus was, "*Do what you must do, but do it while you still can do it, cause when it all comes down to dust, the wind is a-gonna blow through it ...*"

* * *

My best friend in high school was a counselor with me at a Jewish day camp situated at one of the beautiful lakes north of Toronto. On a day off I suggested to him that we hitchhike to a cottage my family used to rent during summers. Somehow we found it off a country road. The family who were there were all out on the lake except for their grandmother. She greeted us as we knocked on the cabin door and invited us in. She talked passionately for a long time, telling us about Jesus and the Devil. As my best friend and I left I told her that I didn't think we had come there by coincidence, to which she whole-heartedly agreed. My friend and I began to walk down the country road to make our way back to our camp before nightfall. Suddenly I noticed that my hand was bleeding and so was his! It was a strange phenomenon. Had we snagged our hands on a bush or tree branch by the side of the road? Was it a further sign that our meeting with the elderly lady was more than a coincidence? To this day I have no explanation for it but I do recall that we both noticed it and wondered what had caused our hands to bleed.

After High School, I knew that I needed to travel to expand my horizons and focus on my spiritual quest for God. I recall sitting with my older sister on our front porch and telling her that I knew God must be out there and that he must want to find us. I felt sure that he was going to find me. With that mindset, I stuffed my T-shirts, with images of my rock'n'roll heroes printed on them, into my backpack and headed to Israel where my maternal grandparents had retired in Jerusalem. I was going to base myself there and then continue to backpack through Europe, allowing my whims to take me from city to city with the unlimited Eurail pass I had purchased.

Chapter 2

From Mount Sinai to Michelangelo

Israel was a wonder to me: a state of my fellow Jewish kinsmen. A state in which *we* were the majority! After getting settled into my room in my grandparents' high-rise apartment in *Rehavia*, Jerusalem, they sent me off on a trip to the Sinai desert which included a climb up the traditional site of Mount Sinai. Our command car (an overgrown jeep) headed out of Jerusalem with a group of European tourists. When we passed Eilat we encountered the stark, vast expanses of the desert ahead of us and glimpses of the sparkling Red Sea on our left side. I was very much a loner and so kept to myself as we made our way to the tip of the Sinai peninsula. I was intrigued by two Swiss women who seemed to always have their Bibles open on their laps as we journeyed.

When we arrived at *Sharm El-Sheikh* we were greeted by our Bedouin guide. We spread out our sleeping bags in the

sand at the base of Mount Sinai near Saint Catherine's Monastery. Tired from our travelling, we lay beneath the stars enjoying the solitude of the desert.

Jostled out of our sleep before dawn, we formed a line and stumbled in silence up the winding mountain ascent. Under a blue-black sky, we followed the beam of light from our Bedouin guide's flashlight. Our guide had timed things so that we arrived at the plateaued mountain peak as the morning's first light broke over the horizon. Hues of bright red and orange beams of light lit up the mountains leaving me breathless. As I gazed across the vast panorama, I thought, "Moses and the children of Israel wandered through this desert. Maybe there's more to Judaism than I realized." I was standing in the place where my ancient ancestors had journeyed when they encountered God in the wilderness. Like a sudden gust of wind that elevates a bird's wings, a sense of hope lifted my spirit. I was on a trail to encounter the God of my forefathers.

* * *

Upon returning to Jerusalem, I said goodbye to Helen, the mystical long-haired olive-skinned religious Jewish girl with deep brown eyes, whose family I had met through my grandparents. I promised her that I'd come back to Israel one day but that I needed to move on to backpack through

Europe. I also promised her that I'd continue my spiritual search in our backyard—our Jewish tradition. On the way to the airport, the cab driver tried to convince me to stay in Israel and said that he could help me check in to an "absorption center." I felt the magnetic pull of the Jewish nation on my soul but knew that there was more of the world I needed to see first. Israel would have to wait while I continued my search for God.

Hanging out at my uncle's apartment in London, I made my way through the city— trying a "bitter" in a pub, watching a new band play in a small club as their lead singer, a short guy from Dublin named "Bono," swung from the chandelier. I stared at melting faces and clocks at an exhibit of Salvador Dali's paintings that reflected a deep inner psychology of our subconscious. How different they were from a life-size charcoal sketch by DaVinci of the "Mother and Child" motif that I gazed in wonder at in London's National Gallery. I think I realized that one of the two babies in the sketch was Jesus but had no knowledge of who the other one was, neither had I heard of "John the Baptist"!

My encounter with Jesus was soon to take on new dimensions as I made my way through Europe by train and ended up in Rome. On the way there I decided to stop in Interlaken, a resort town nestled in the mountains of central Switzerland. As I was standing outside a bank I heard a cheerful voice gleefully call out to me, "Hello!" Lo and behold, it was one of the Swiss "Bible ladies" who had been part of our Sinai desert tour. "This is amazing, that we should meet here!" She went on to explain to me that she only came to Interlaken once a week to do her banking and thus concluded the providential nature of our encounter. She invited me to come back with her to her chalet for lunch. After enjoying a nice meal and viewing her photographs of our Sinai trip, she shared her faith in Jesus with me and then took me back to Interlaken. As I got out of her car she handed me a book. "Here, this is for you." I thanked her, waved goodbye, and looked at the book's title, *Death of a Guru.* I stuck it in my backpack and returned to my hostel.

The next morning, I made my way up a mountain by train taking in the picturesque scenery. When the train reached its stop high above the town, I felt that my transcendent location, alone in the mountains, seemed to be a good place to offer a prayer. I prayed to the God of my forefathers, Abraham, Isaac, and Jacob, "God, please show me if Jesus is our Messiah." There was no voice from heaven, and I was not even sure if God, who I assumed was out there somewhere, had even heard my prayer.

A few days later, at the Florence train station, I began reading the book my Swiss friend had given me. All I recall is that it was about a Brahmin priest and his encounter with Jesus, who, he related, "appeared to him." I felt that it was way too "out there" for me and chucked it into a dustbin as I waited for my train.

Arriving in Rome, I felt dwarfed by Saint Peter's gigantic promenade leading to its entrance. I had no inkling that the huge cement statues standing atop the basilica's façade were *Jewish* men—including Jesus, himself, and some of his apostles, most of whom lived by the Sea of Galilee which I had just visited. Before leaving Jerusalem, I had grabbed a book from my grandmother's bookshelf, titled, *The Agony and the Ecstasy*—a historical fiction of Michelangelo's life. I had just read about the life-size sculpture that he chiseled from a huge slab of white marble. I had no idea that I was about to encounter it.

As I entered the basilica, my eyes fell upon Michelangelo's famous *Pieta.* I was equally amazed and confused as I approached it. Why was the mysterious white marble man lying on this melancholy woman's lap? My eyes focused upon the holes in his hands, side, and feet. I didn't have any categories to understand what I was looking at. Despite my disorientation, I felt strangely drawn to the image. A mysterious sense of sacred peace seemed to emanate from the dead man's body.

After finally pulling myself away, I made my way into the Sistine Chapel. Above my head was the iconic floating image of God, imparting life to Adam with his divine finger. My gaze then shifted to the mind-dazzling fresco on the far wall of the chapel. A man was sitting on a throne two-thirds up the wall. His majestic muscular frame and his serious demeanor showed that he meant business. He seemed to be engaged in some kind of apocalyptic judgment. Above him, angels were escorting people to the celestial realm. Below him, dark demonic figures were yanking poor souls with anguished expressions down into *Sheol* (i.e., the after-world, Hell). At the bottom of the fresco, a Dantean-like demon in a boat was ferrying some poor souls across a river to their impending doom.

Disoriented and dazed, I stood there frozen in time, attempting to take in the power of the image before me. Again I realized that I did not have categories with which I could make sense of this epic scene. What now seems so obvious hit my consciousness with a thud. The *man* sitting on the throne was one of *us*, a *Jew*. I knew that it was Jesus and was amazed that a Jewish man had made such an overwhelming impact on European Christian culture.

IONAS

Years later I wrote a poem of my experience standing in front of Michelangelo's iconic pieta and then beholding his giant fresco. At the beginning of my poem, I refer to the huge sentry-like statues that stand atop St. Peter's Basilica. As I noted, I had no idea at the time that most of these towering men were Jewish fishermen who became—growing in size and fame over time—the famous apostles of the Church. In the second part of the poem, I mention the painter Raphael, who, while painting his masterpieces at the time, managed to have someone unlock the door of the Sistine Chapel to see the majestic painting of his rival, and as a result, revised his painting style.

A Jewish Backpacker's Stop at St. Peter's Basilica and the Sistine Chapel

Galilean sentries stationed over
Rome, from your lake-side village how you've
grown, and grown, and grown. Your sculptured forms
suspended soak the sun of centuries past, in this

imposing courtyard where the faithful come
for Mass. Inside your master humbly waits for
souls to come and contemplate. What is this
burning fire that my bones cannot contain?

How does this cold white marble transmit heat
within my veins? And tell me Michelangelo,
this mystery must I know, How has your chisel
wrought such wonders that my spirit feels wind

blow? Far from friends and home, one feels so frail
and alone, but why does my heart here feel
such a piercing ache? My eyes behold an
image that my words cannot relate? Is

this some ancient prophecy that has
since been fulfilled? And Miriam, why do
you sit serene, resigned, and still? A mother's
heart seeks to embrace her children in her arms,

but on your lap a corpse is laid; and why
has he been harmed? Why are his hands
and feet and side pierced through with nail holes?
Such pain, and grief, and sadness flowing from your
mother's soul?

I drag myself
away, as if to gain release from some
unworldly peace that tugs upon my heart
and bids me stay ...

* * *

Raphael, please tell me how you felt
when stealthily you crept inside, and dumb
and dazzled knelt? And when you saw his paint,
Did you conclude he was a man or that he was a saint?

My heart tells me, despite
my fear, my steps were surely guided here;
then Charon calls to ferry me across
this gloomy way — I shudder and perspire

as screams rise from icy fire. Christ enthroned!
Majestic arm raised powerful and daunting.
Somehow my soul inwardly knows that its
been weighed and is found wanting. I plead for

mercy in my simple way, for Sabbath
School did not at all prepare me for the
Judgment Day.

Sabbath school did not at all prepare
me for this day ...

Chapter 3

Toronto, Torah, and Transcendence

Back in my basement room, my wall was now decorated with a poster of the Mona Lisa, which I had seen in the Louvre. I thought that perhaps some illumination might emanate from the iconic painting to lift my soul to a higher plane. I had collected a stack of about fifty postcards during my Museum visits in Europe—each one displaying a famous painting that I had seen up close. I delivered Pizzas to earn some pocket money but my passion was music. I spent hours playing songs on my acoustic guitar. I soaked myself in folk and blues music and tried my best to channel Dylan with my blues harp propped up from my neck as I strummed away singing, *Hey, Mr. Tambourine Man.*

Next, it was time to keep my promise to Helen, the mysterious girl from Jerusalem. I had sat beside an orthodox Jew on a flight from NYC to Toronto. He provided me with the address of an adult Jewish learning center in Toronto. As I sat listening to the teacher riff about "Torah," and sundry comments about fulfilling the "mitzvot" (commandments) in marriage, something stirred in me. I followed that prompting and agreed to visit a venerable elderly rabbi. The white-bearded Rabbi was delighted that a lost sheep was coming home. He arranged for me to spend the Shabbat with an orthodox Jewish family. As part of my spiritual preparation for the Shabbat visit, I read a book that he had given me about Marrano Jews. These were Spanish Jews who were forced to convert to Catholicism but remained crypto-Jews. The carved image of Mary on their doorposts secretly served as a Mezuzah (Jewish ritual parchment of Hebrew Bible verses rolled up in an encased scroll). They also lit Shabbat candles in rooms without windows. I began to feel the fire inside of me that I took to be the fire of my Jewish soul returning home. The rabbi later explained to me that I felt this way because my soul was present with *Am Yisrael* (the people of Israel) when we stood at Mount Sinai and heard God thunder the words of Torah when He established His covenant with us.

Accompanied by a couple of young observant Jewish men, I sat at the Sabbath table of the orthodox family who was hosting us. The sacred peace that seemed to accompany the soft light of the sabbath candles amidst ancient prayers made a deep impression on me. On another visit to the

Jewish study center, I recall, on my way home my small car skidded on the icy road. As it spun back on course, avoiding an accident, I was sure that *HaShem* (*The Name,* i.e., God) was watching out for me. I tried to get our family to observe a more traditional Friday night Sabbath meal but soon realized they did not share my newfound zeal to embrace a deeper level of Judaism's spirituality.

This season of life was a lonely one. Adding to my sense of something that seemed missing in my life, was a lack of stability in our home life at the time. My beloved father and I were very close. He was larger than life to my siblings and me. He was tall, handsome, charming, and an outstanding athlete. He was a world-class runner in his youth and ran at Israel's Maccabee games, Israel's Jewish version of the Olympics. However, he had run into business troubles that caused tension in our family and eventually led to our parents' divorce, and my dad's decision to return to South Africa. I tried to process our family breakdown and my dad's departure stoically and protect my heart from life's pain as I continued to search for inner peace.

My romance with Judaism had hit a wall. Although I was sure that I had discovered a true spark of spirituality in traditional Judaism, it did not seem like it was going to provide me with the personal connection with God that I was searching for. I called the elderly rabbi who had become a sort of spiritual counselor to me and explained to him that I needed to look elsewhere for my spiritual connection with God. He responded by telling me that I needed to be more patient. By developing a heightened '*kavanah*' (deep concentration) in my prayers I would attain the deeper connection I was seeking. I thanked him for his counsel and assured him that I would always remain Jewish but insisted, nonetheless, that I felt I had to look outside Judaism's traditional path to find that connection. His tone let me know that he was exasperated by my decision and he promptly ended the phone call. All that I found attractive in traditional Judaism would one day come back to me in a new form, but for now, my path became the Eastern one.

I had moved out of home and was renting an apartment in mid-town Toronto. I worked as a waiter at a trendy dessert coffee shop. I felt at home with the young crowd that worked there, who were all artsy types on spiritual journeys of one sort or another. Furthermore, the owner was a middle-aged man who had the disposition of a type of older brother to many of us. He had a great sense of humor and a good work ethic and was deeply committed to the Eastern path. He was eager to share his understanding of Eastern spirituality with me. After reading a book on meditation that he gave me, I set out to "test the waters" of my new path.

As I sat cross-legged in a nearby park, I slowly breathed in and then exhaled, imagining the color of my breath as a deep blue cloud spreading from my lungs, out my mouth, and into the atmosphere. Then a red cloud, then a purple, one, then a pink one, etc. This was one of the first Eastern spiritual exercises that I learned, all connected to my *kundalini*—the purported spiritual power source at the base of one's spine, and the portal to the spiritual world.

Before landing on the Eastern path I had "done the rounds" of spiritual options at my doorstep in downtown Toronto. My first stop was the office of the Scientology religion, founded by Ron Hubbard. After counseling with a spiritual guide, he led me to a table where I held onto two tube-like objects attached to some sort of meter that moved a needle in front of my *auditor*. As my memory faintly recalls, I proceeded to answer a series of questions — which process they call "auditing"— so that I could get "pre-clear" on my path to the spiritual enlightenment on offer. As I walked out of the Scientology offices and joined the flow of life on Yonge St., Toronto's main north-south artery, I felt a sigh of relief that I could check off Scientology from my list. If I gained any clarity from my "auditing" it was that Scientology seemed to be more of a spiritual hoax than the path that would lead me to the living God.

My next stop was a Church building downtown that was being used as a Hindu temple. I walked in and saw the statue of Krishna—or, whatever Hindu god was being presented. The 'god' had a necklace of flowers around its neck and, along with incense, there were various offerings that had been placed by its side. That was all I needed to see before doing a U-turn out of the building. Whatever Jewish sensibilities towards monotheism I had, or simply basic spiritual intuitions, 'Hinduism' and its devotion to idols could not, I reasoned, be the true revelation of God. Ironically, as my story played out, I ended up on the Eastern path.

I was now living with a fellow employee in the Greek area of downtown Toronto. I continued to develop my connection with the artsy crowd I was hanging with and met a beautiful, tall Chinese girl and her 'punk' boyfriend who seemed to be a local version of a disgruntled Sid Vicious, the lead singer of the Sex Pistols. His girlfriend had asked me if I sang, and before I knew it, I found myself auditioning in front of her boyfriend. After strumming my guitar and channeling some Dylan, Kinks, and Bowie songs, he asked me, "But what is *your* voice?" His question caught me off-guard and confronted me with the realization that, whatever my voice was, I had not yet found it. Nonetheless, he figured I'd do the job, and I began rehearsing his songs. He played electric guitar and his girlfriend played electric bass. After rehearsing for several weeks they got a gig at a downtown club. I invited a couple of friends to come and watch me "perform." After listening to a funk band play and its lead singer jive to their songs—I was thinking, "Wow, this guy is good, how am I going to get up there and sing after him?" But I made my way up to the elevated stage with my friends and saw a drummer whom we had not yet rehearsed with, whom they had enlisted for the performance. I looked out at the crowd, sitting around circular tables, and approached the mic as the drummer banged out a powerful beat in time with the lead guitar player's raunchy chords. I felt the drum beats vibrating through my whole being as I belted out the lyrics. By now I had long red hair and so I guess I somewhat looked the part, despite my lack of a strong stage presence. This short-lived "punk" band experience contributed to my spiritual journey. One of the songs the band leader had written was called, "Praise Jesus." I still recall some of the lyrics. "*See me walking down the street with a smile on my face … I used to be ******-up on drugs, Praise Jesus now I'm ******-up on God.*" Even though I had a powerful spiritual experience at St. Peter's, I still had not made a clear connection between Jesus and God. As I was rehearsing this song for the first time, whose conceit was mocking formal religion and specifically, Christianity, I had a very tangible impression that a voice was whispering to my spirit, "Don't," as in "Don't sing this song." I felt a strong conviction at the time that I was violating something or someone sacred by singing it but simply chose to ignore the "voice" and my conscience and went ahead with the gig, as I have related. So ended my inglorious, and irreverent "rock star" career.

Despite my negative experience with the Hindu idol I had stumbled upon, I still saw the Eastern path as the most promising one and surrounded myself with like-minded souls. I discovered an *Ashram* (and Eastern Path spiritual/meditation center) not far from my house apartment on Bloor St. East (the Greek cultural area of Toronto). The particular Ashram that I started visiting was run by devotees of Maharaji (not to be confused with the Beatles' famous guru, Maharishi Mahesh Yogi). Maharaji made his first appearance in the USA at the age of thirteen. I began to attend the Ashram regularly and listened to devotional "talks" given by its leaders, and was intrigued by an Indian woman who showed up at one of our sessions and prostrated herself to worship—I assumed in honor of the guru.

After a season of hanging out with the leadership of the Ashram and seeking spiritual enlightenment, I was becoming anxious. One night, around midnight, my desperation sent me walking over to the Ashram and knocking on the door. When the surprised hostess opened the door and recognized me, I blurted out, "I want to be initiated *now*." She led me to a room and instructed me how to place my thumbs in my ears to listen to the "drums," and repeat my newly given mantra. Despite my initial feeling of excitement over hearing what seemed to be a soft and constant conga-drum type tapping in my ears, after a couple of hours of repeating my mantra, a sinking feeling began to overwhelm me. I had a clear sense that I was not going to "receive" enlightenment. I quietly let myself out of the Ashram and headed home. Even though I was disappointed that my "initiation" did not lead to a deep spiritual experience, I still believed that the Eastern path would lead me to God.

Not long after this time, a sense of spiritual suffocation overtook me. I felt that I needed to "escape" the temptation of drifting into a complacent social and professional life in Toronto that would dampen the spiritual spark in my soul and my search for God. I decided that I would travel to South Africa to continue my spiritual search there and reconnect with my dad.

Chapter 4

From Johannesburg to Cape Town—Finding Peace at Last

It was great to be together with my father again. Despite his loneliness, he was doing much better and was grateful for my presence in his life again. Before long, I was hanging out with my uncle and aunt who lived in Johannesburg. My aunt was a yoga teacher (her garage was a Yoga studio) and she was hard-core on the Eastern Path. We both felt a strong spiritual connection and a common spiritual "language." Before long, she had convinced me to abandon the guru I had adopted in Toronto and to switch to her guru, Rajneesh. (A Netflix film on his life and the controversies surrounding him was released in 2018).

After spending time with family in Johannesburg, I flew to Durban, to hitchhike to Cape Town. I headed out with my guitar, songbooks, a book of Rajneesh's teaching, a backpack, and a tent. The burning flame in my soul continued to drive me to find the enlightenment I was seeking. On one of my stops along the way in a camping park, I came out of my tent to greet the morning sun in the lotus position to begin meditating. Instead of a sense of spiritual progress, however, I had the distinct and depressing feeling that something was blocking my attempts to gain enlightenment but I had no idea what it was.

A kind soul stopped to give me a ride as I hitchhiked towards the Cape. I felt free and full of hope as we sailed along the coastal highway, the wind blowing my long hair in his open truck bed. As the sun lowered on the horizon, we came over a ridge revealing a panoramic view of Cape Town. The city was sprawled like a jewel in the shape of a circular valley that led to its beaches bordering the intersection of the Atlantic and Indian oceans. My heart was overwhelmed and refreshed by the site of Cape Town and the scent of fresh sea air.

Before long I found myself settled in and working in a record store. When the co-owners—two Jewish kinsmen—interviewed me for the job, they smiled with amusement when I explained to them that I was a "post-punk" youth. This was 1981, which was still the era of LPs which the store "rented" to its customers. After opening the store one morning, I decided to put on a Dylan album. After flipping through his discography, I was intrigued to find his most recent album titled, *Saved.* As the track, *In the Garden,* played, I was gripped by its lyrics and Dylan's sense of love and reverence for Jesus. The song tells the story of Jesus's arrest in the garden of Gethsemane.

When they came for Him in the garden, did they know? Did they know He was the Son of God, did they know that He was Lord? Did they hear when He told Peter, "Peter, put up your sword?" When they came for Him in the garden, did they know?... Nicodemus came at night so he wouldn't be seen by men Saying, "Master, tell me why a man must be born again. ... When He healed the blind and crippled, did they see? When He said, "Pick up your bed and walk, why must you criticize? Same thing My Father do, I can do likewise." ... When He rose from the dead, did they believe? He said, "All power is given to Me in heaven and on earth." Did they know right then and there what that power was worth?[1]

Around that time, an attractive woman, named Trudy, came into the store. I went over to the section of LPs that she was flipping through and asked if I could help her find something. I showed her an album that had an Eastern theme cover on it and she simply said, "Oh, no thanks, I'm not into that." When I asked her what she was "into," she replied, "Jesus." Before I knew it she showed up at the store again with the gift of a Bible for me. I thanked her for it,

---

[1] Copyright © 1980 by Special Rider Music.

but when I tried reading it at the apartment where I was staying, it was a closed book to me. I didn't feel I could understand or relate to it at all. I put it into a drawer and left it there.

I loved going down to the beach in the late afternoon to enjoy the beauty of Cape Town's stunning sunsets. As I was taking in that beauty one day, a young man walked over to greet me. As we talked, he began to tell me about Jesus and added that he felt led to stop his car to come over to tell me about him. I explained to him that I already had a guru, not one from two thousand years ago, but a living one for our own time. Nonetheless, the books I was then reading by Eastern spiritual guides often quoted Jesus's sayings, and I was intrigued by them. For example, (from the Gospel of Matthew, Chapter 6),

Do not be anxious about your life, what you will eat or what you will drink, nor about your body, what you will put on. Is not life more than food, and the body more than clothing? Look at the birds of the air: they neither sow nor reap nor gather into barns, and yet your heavenly Father feeds them. Are you not of more value than they?

I agreed to let him pray for me and then watched him walk off into the distance. Soon afterward, Trudy was back in my record shop inviting me to visit her church. My decision to agree was not unconnected to the light that I sensed emanating from her. She was a kind and shining soul and I was already beginning to think that she might also be a sort of guardian angel sent to help me on my quest for God.

I was amazed to see some of the merchants at church, whom I had previously run into from various stores I had frequented in town. They also seemed to shine the same light and peace that I saw in Trudy. As the congregation lifted their hands and sang, I thought there was perhaps someone at the front of the church to whom they were expressing their devotion. As I continued to visit their meetings, I eventually understood that they were worshiping Jesus, whom they believed was alive and would one day return to earth.

As I was walking on the streets of Sea Point, Cape Town one afternoon, an African woman came over and greeted me. Before long our conversation turned to spiritual things. When I told her that I was Jewish, she took me by the hand and brought me to an apartment of a Jewish man where a small group of Jewish people were meeting with a Gentile pastor. He was teaching them about Jesus in the Old Testament (the Hebrew Bible). I was amazed by the things he was teaching us and also glad to meet other Jewish souls who were seeking to know more about Jesus. One man in particular made a deep impression on me. He told me how he was once in a synagogue, standing in front of the ark (where the Torah Scroll is kept), when, under his breath, he cursed God. He related to me, how at that same moment he felt a surge of an electric-like shock go through his body. It was, apparently, God's way of warning him and letting him know that He is the true and living God.

I also had some powerful experiences at the church services at this time. God was exposing the darkness in me. I began to sense His holiness and my sinfulness and felt compelled to run out of the service. These experiences had a cumulative effect on my soul. I saw my life flashing before my eyes. I got out of my lotus position and onto my knees and cried out to God. I had finally understood that the thing that was blocking my path to God was my sin and rebellion against Him.

At this time I was hanging out with some of the young adults who attended the church. One of the young men from this group asked me if I had said "the sinner's prayer." I had no idea what that was but agreed, nonetheless, to repeat it after him. "Lord, God, I come to You as a sinner and thank You for sending Jesus to die for my sins on the cross. I repent of my sins and choose to follow You and submit my life to You as my Lord and Savior."

I didn't give much thought to the prayer when I returned to my apartment. However, I felt a desire to read the Bible I had stored away in a drawer. As I read it, I was overcome with excitement as I realized that I not only understood what I was reading but that God was my Heavenly Father, and that He was speaking to me through His Word. I knew that Jesus was the long-awaited Jewish Messiah, whose image had so struck my heart in the Basilica of Rome and the Sistine Chapel.

Shortly after that, I ended up staying in a sort of commune-house with several young people who were all on the Eastern path. One night, before going to sleep, I felt a burning conviction to take a sheet of paper and write on it the words of Jesus from the Gospel of John that had become so precious to me, "*I am the Way, the Truth, and the Life.*" I knew that in that spiritual atmosphere, there was a strong sense of oppression against Jesus's exclusive claim. I placed the paper sign above the living room mantel. In the morning, I was not surprised to see that it had been taken down.

At that time I met an older couple in Cape Town whom someone had connected me with. The wife was a Jewish believer. When I met her I was so happy to find another Jewish person who believed in Jesus as our Messiah. She showed me Isaiah, chapter 53, and I was amazed to see that God had provided such a detailed chapter in our own Hebrew Bible about Jesus and his sacrifice for our sins.

He was pierced for our transgressions;
he was crushed for our iniquities;
upon him was the chastisement that brought us peace,
and with his wounds we are healed.
All we like sheep have gone astray;
we have turned—every one—to his own way;
and the LORD has laid on him
the iniquity of us all.

I spent the next few months traveling with a small group of young people, packed into a car, selling Encyclopedias to families in small community towns from Cape Town to Johannesburg. After I would finish my sales pitch to the family who had let me in their home, I would often ask if they had received the "free gift." When they said, "no," I would proceed to share with them that Jesus is the free gift that God has given us. Many of those to whom I made my sales presentation were Christians, and I was delighted to enjoy spending some time with them sharing our common faith and love for God before heading out to the next home on the street.

When I arrived in Johannesburg and shared my new faith with my grandma Janie, she surprised me by telling me that we had a family member who also believed in Jesus. I soon met my "aunt Maize," a sweet elderly woman who told me that she had been praying for my family for fifty years. She had an amazing story of how, as a young orthodox Jewish girl, she had come to faith in Jesus as her Messiah. She had a chronic sickness as a teenager, and when she allowed a pastor visiting the hospital to pray for her, she was miraculously healed. She would later tell me that her faith in Jesus was also the result of a winsome Christian school friend who made a deep impression on her. When she came home with her new faith her younger sister shook her by the neck saying, "How could you do this to mom?"

Maize later related to me how that same evening, as she lay on her bed staring at the ceiling, she said, "God, I believe that Jesus is my Messiah and want to follow Him, but I can't break my mother's heart." At that moment a light flashed in her room and she audibly heard God say, "Follow me." And follow Him she did. She never married, fasted every other day, and dedicated herself to sharing the Good News of Messiah with the South African Jewish community. She led many of them to a saving knowledge of Jesus as their Messiah. I have met two Israelis from South Africa who have told me that they came to faith because of her. She had a bumper sticker on the back of her car, *"The life of the flesh is in the blood, I have given it to you upon the altar to make atonement for your souls"* Leviticus 17:11," and below it a reference to the Talmud, (*Yoma* 5a) that says the same thing.

Aunt Maize was a godsend for my life. She was able to answer all my questions about Jesus and also introduced me to a precious group of mostly elderly "Hebrew Christians," who held a monthly meeting in Johannesburg. Maize later came to my wedding in Jaffa, Israel, and then went on to receive her heavenly reward. More than her impressive knowledge of God and His Word, the light that shone from her, and her love and dedication to God continue to inspire me.

I have written this story of my journey of faith more than forty years after I became a believer in Yeshua (Jesus). He truly has become the supreme love of my life, my closest friend, and my Messiah and Savior. He gave His life and precious blood for me and for you, to die for our sins and grant us the gift of forgiveness, spiritual rebirth, and everlasting life.

I leave you with His invitation from the Gospel of Matthew. His arms are open to receive you and give you the joy of knowing that you are the object of His love. God loves you so much that He sent His only Son, Jesus, to die in your place so that you can enjoy His friendship in this life, and life everlasting in the world to come.

Come to me, all you who are weary
and are carrying heavy burdens,
and I will give you rest.

* * *

www.ingramcontent.com/pod-product-compliance
Lightning Source LLC
LaVergne TN
LVHW041254150826
845673LV00008B/2586

* 9 7 8 2 9 1 3 4 4 4 9 8 0 *